Beginning to Figure Things Out

Beginning to Figure Things Out

Poems by

Craig Bruce McVay

Cover design by Shay Culligan

ISBN: 978-1-63980-230-2

Kelsay Books
502 South 1040 East, A-119
American Fork, Utah 84003
Kelsaybooks.com

For my wife, Sue Burnam

With thanks to Linda Fuller-Smith, who helped edit the book, and to friends in the Columbus workshops, Episcopal Poets and Salon

Acknowledgments

The poems below, including some revisions, appeared first in the following publications:

Atticus Review: "The Husband Approaches Morning in Maine"

Calliope: "Depression Comes Again and Grabs You from Behind"

Common Threads: "Love on a Sunday Afternoon"

Everything Stops and Listens (anthology, Ohio Poetry Association)*:* "Dogwood on the Hill"

FishFood Magazine: "The Little Boy Hides from the Ugly Man"

Grey Sparrow: "Autumn Comes to Indiana," "Looking for Grace's New Birthday Spoon in the Dumpster at the Back of the School," "Silently Toward the River"

Pudding Magazine: "Execution"

Quiet Diamonds: "At Summer's End," "Grotesqueries of Death: Students in the Catacombs of Rome"

Shot-Glass Journal: "Principal Parts," "Stepfather at Dinner"

Tipton Petry Journal: "The Poet Faces the Dawn"

Tule Review: "The Wall"

The Write Room: "Trigger"

Contents

The Wall

As I write my story, a poem
crouches on cracked haunches
on the shadowed side of the wall.

I walk in step with the story.
It's friendly, and we talk.

My pen paints whispering paragraphs
on impermeable black stones.
First. Then. Finally.

I stop and stoop and lean against the wall,
listening hard for the poem to show itself.

My right ear roughens ragged and ruddy:
I want to hear the earth and air shake
as my poem stands—slowly, I imagine—
plants its feet, breathes twice,
then dips, swings its elbows
and jumps.

I want to see my poem dance, rhythmically,
as it comes over and to see my pen dance
sun-red with it.

As my poem rises, I want my story to smile,
even if sadly, and go rest quietly
in the leaves.

Grotesqueries of Death: Students in the Catacombs of Rome

We marched slowly through narrow
tunnels of stacked papal bones and skulls,
where Mother told me once the early
Christians hid and died and rose.

We were young enough to know
that we would never know
the grotesqueries of death.

Most of us were friends. Most.
As some smiled and whispered, silence
like a stone pressed on my tongue. I spoke,
as if in prayer, to no one. And I began
to cry.

Once a nice Methodist boy, I was now
a Doubting Thomas (though afraid to touch
Jesus' wounds): Will we live beyond death?

Near us, in the Protestant cemetery, lay Keats.
Quietly his stone sang, *Here lies
one whose name was writ in water.*

We were far from the Indiana graveyard,
next to the field where teenagers hid among
July's green tassels and kissed.

In the church, we sang, *How Lovely
Is Thy Dwelling Place.*

Crying, I told the priest in stumbling words,

My mother is dead.

Depression Comes again and Grabs You
from Behind

You ride breakneck into the woods.
Your red 10-speed, handlebars like rams' horns,
dances through October slants of light

when you hear the limber wraith
you thought was gone
racing on his snorting pony after you.

He throws a gray hood over your head
and the woods go dark and the black roots
grab your tires and throw you over the handlebars,

and your mangled bike, silent as a slaughtered
kid, tongue black and eyes bulging, lies
beside you.

Love on a Sunday Afternoon

Giggling,
they take turns playing
on each other's bellies.

They kiss curly hair under the sheet.

The flies on the ceiling
don't bother them.

They love slowly, like the spreading
blue sedge in low woods
at the edges of meadows.

Baling Hay in Indiana

We're standing on the wagon,
Bobby and I, knees bent slightly and
balancing as if ready for a ground ball.
We're at Mr. Browne's today, and his black
Percherons, Lovely Lady and Whispering
Belle, plod along.

They lean their faces into each other,
chuckling over secrets. Mr. Browne turns
around every so often. Grinning like a grandpa,
he calls, *Aren't they beautiful, boys!*

He doesn't drive like Mr. Lemmon, whose
shotgun tractor whips loud through the fields,
and we have to run and lift and stack the bales
over our heads or maybe we even get shaken
off the wagon like I did once. Bobby pulled
me back. He's got a better arm than me,
and that's why he's the shortstop and I
play second.

Why Mr. Browne still farms with horses,
nobody knows, but we like lifting their black
harnesses of a morning and watching them
float like quilts onto their quivering backs.

Sometimes Mr. Browne lets us ride, like proud
cavalrymen, to the field. If he meets somebody
on the road, he laughs and calls us horse flies.
He has a few cows, too, but none of them
have names.

Mr. Lemmon only scowls and yells, like an angry
crow stung under its wings by wasps. People
say he used to beat his kids to the ground before
they got away.

Mrs. Browne comes and brings us chicken
and mayonnaise sandwiches. She's twenty
years younger than Mr. Browne, with long
red hair grinning over her forehead.

They got married last month when
her bump began to show. They laugh,
and nobody talks mean.

Everybody's glad she got away from
that ugly man's belt, and they say it's too
bad her mama can't leave him, but
all her family is dead.

Bobby and I talk about Mrs. Browne
on our way home. We've both kissed girls,
but we're scared to try anything more—as if
they would let us, anyway.

We wonder what it would be like to go
all the way, and we laugh and figure
we'd never even get to second base.

The Little Boy Climbs into Another World

Lazing by the east pasture of fescue,
I stare at the giant white crow, whose black
eyes stare back.

His gold and black claws clench the rusted
barbed wire. His staccato rattle calls me,
and I stand and climb the fence, which jabs
and tears the palms of my hands.

Now a friend, bleeding, I follow him
as he dances across the pasture, where we see
the two white bulls that follow the black
heifer and mount her, one then the other.

We watch her eagerly, months later, as she
lies on her side in the west pasture, chained
to the fence to which the crow and I fly.

We see the bare left arm of the scowling
farmer disappear inside her. We hear
her shout as the yellow water, then the legs,
appear.

Clinging to the fence, the crow and I cackle—
he more loudly than I—at the moaning mother
and her silent black calf as the flies play
in the brown matted circle of ragweed.

Black County, Indiana

What if midnight black remains black?
What if slanted sleet pains the farmhouse?

What if the pump draws rusty water?
What if the jagged crack wrestles door from post?

What if the heater warms half the kitchen?
What if the dishwater goes swampy?

What if the door of the ice box falls?
What if the hot meat rots?

What if mud drowns the floor?
What if the chamber pot stinks full?

What if paint crashes from the wall?
What if tape yellows the windows?

What if barbed wire lies in the weeds?
What if a calf bawls at the surging dirty red?

What if a farmer lies in the mud-matted straw?
What if a mob of crows surrounds him?

Principal Parts

We lie in bed, and I lie to you.

You say you love the clarity with which I speak,
that my silent kisses whisper in your ear.

We lay together last night, and I lied to you.

You said my words warmed your breath
and ran naked as night through your hair.

We have lain together often, and every night
I have lied.

And you've told me my words streamed
over your breast like silver water in the spring.

My dear, listen closely.
I shall lie and lie again. And you will say
I love you.

Trigger

Christmas afternoon
and hard by the trail of black smoke
that smelled like the tannery across town,
the little boy was beginning to figure things out.

Yesterday before dark, Daddy
brought the boots, polished a deep oxblood,
and set them—
Trigger painted proudly on the sides—
under the tree. Then
he went home.

Next morning,
Mama announced cowboy boots pinch your toes.

Her new boyfriend said so.

She dragged brush to the burn pile,
struck a match
and hurled the boots into the flames.
They lay sole pressing on sole.

The melting and streaking polish gagged her.

Every few minutes,
with all the eloquence a four-year-old
could muster,
the little boy begged,
Please, Mama, please.

The smoke hovered contentedly,
like wild horses milling and grazing in the scrub
until they smell trouble.
Holding still, quivering,
they receive the arrows in their necks.

Too close to the pile, the little boy gagged
and smelled
the sadness that was Trigger,
bridled, bit in mouth,
waiting with no protest for the knacker.

Execution

The rabbit
he raps once on the head
with a two-by-four
before he ties
its feet to the line
and settles his knife
into warm fur.

The rooster
he grabs in his fist
and hangs still cursing
while he saws
at its neck.

Why?

To make little boys
ask questions.

The Little Boy Hides from the Ugly Man

Hope settles
like a summer peach
in the little boy's stomach
as he dives under the bed.

The man snarls and tears
through the shorts and tee-shirts
on the floor of the boy's closet. His face
is gnarled like the cane he grips.

Foolish as a five-year-old can be,
the little boy laughs. Mortal laughter.
Wrenched by the arm, he begins to cry
before the fire starts to dance on his red back.

The man does not smell his own ugly stink.

The boy cries too hard to ask why his mother
won't put a stop to this.

Stepfather at Dinner

Sitting,
arms so large
crossed against bare chest
pulling his shoulders down
as he leans over the table.

Eyes tiny, tearing at the air,
he sends his silence
crashing down
against us.

The Old Man's Funeral

Jesus knocking at the door, image from
The Light of the World, oil by William
Holman Hunt, ca. 1851

Trudging on stocky legs down the aisle
in new black shoes that blister her heels, Mother
screams forty years of sorrow and anger. Howell,
the only son who has come, clutches her elbow
in the palm of his spider-white hand.

Eyes are on nothing but the two. No one sees
the snow beating at the scratched stained-glass
or Jesus knocking on the door. No one looks at
the old man and his coffin.

No one has seen Howell since the night Mother
sat bawling in the kitchen: *Put away the belt,
please, please,* she begged her husband until
the boy slammed the black storm door and stalked
into a seven-years' night.

Everyone stares at the scar that sulks under
the rag of his beard.

At the coffin, mother and son stand rigid. As
she lowers her head, perhaps to pray, Howell
bends as if to kiss the forehead of the father
he knows he ought to forgive.

But he wants only to pull open and spit
into the ugly man's eyes.

The Husband Approaches Morning in Maine

So, what if one Sunday morning in February,
the sun slants into the kitchen
as you're pouring her coffee
before you settle in with the *Times?*

And you close your eyes
and the snow you saw a minute ago
is white sand on the Mediterranean.

Bare-breasted women rest in canvas chairs,
eyes closed, under parasols.

Or maybe they're reading—
something light, certainly not Dante,
though for years they've meant to finish
the *Paradiso.*

But you know your wife's breasts
are as white, on a winter morning,
as theirs are brown in summer.

Your eyes are still blue.

No One Hears Her Laughing

Mrs. Hill, dying and laughing,
soothes herself with dreams.

No one hears her laughing.

The ladies hold her, near to choking.
They covet and clutch her gown,
rich gold and black, neck now torn.

In the barn, Mr. Hill hammers
square nails into the wooden coffin.
The rhythm of the work,
its purposefulness, comforts him.

Mrs. Hill, dying and laughing,
soothes herself with dreams.

No one hears her laughing.

Outside in the snow,
a brown rabbit sits silently.

Silently toward the River

The builder, driving the black Percherons,
hauls the gray wood from the fallen
round barn to the edge of the river.

Walking slowly behind, the son carries
oats in the bucket that lay, rusting,
next to the pump on the back porch.

The daughter throws the dishwater into the weeds,
then fixes the bread-and-butter sandwiches
she'll take them for supper.

They don't talk about the brown nail
that stuck through Mother's right hand
last fall and locked her jaw for good.

Autumn Comes to Indiana

Today is Sunday.
August winds sing through the red leaves
of the sorrel trees on the ridge out back.

I remember Grace that Sunday night when
we sat in canvas chairs in the back yard.

She was six and starting school the next day
and wondered if she would like her teacher.

That night, Grace learned to snap her fingers.

That night, I told Grace the story of how the ruby
throated hummingbirds ride on the backs
of geese across the moon.

Autumn was come to Indiana,
and Grace was with me.

Looking for Grace's New Birthday Spoon
in the Dumpster at the Back of the School

Diving into the Stygian muck,
searching for the elusive cursive *G*
on the handle of the spoon,
I searched the darkness—

Like a man aching for a daughter,
or a little girl for a daddy.

In the river of deep sadness lay the nameless ghost
of the child we never spoke of.

Swim, I heard her whisper, swim

So I swam, eyes open to the stinking black,
crying under water.

All I could do was grab at grasses of love
that whirled like necrotic skin sloughing from imprecise arms
to try to trace the curving white line of what I would do for her
as long as my breath held.

We huddled to the car.
Grace, as quietly as a river gives up its fog,
pulled my face down and kissed me on the cheek.

The Poet Faces the Dawn

Blind, she pulls on jeans and shirt as frozen
winds squeeze between the skinny brown slats
of the back door. She sees only the dark
meant for no one but her.

> She is alone but for the rancid memories
> of friends with whom she'll never speak again.
> Friends who coiled and spat at her because
> she told the truth.

She drinks the stink of the rusty water she pumped
last night and, with her brown knuckled hands,
washes the dishes from supper. Cold wind
smacks her back.

> She wishes the ghosts of her parents would
> come see her. Questions beg for answers.
> Why did they leave her with the ugly aunt?
> Why did they take her brother, but not her?

The Dogwood on the Hill

No one has pruned the branches
of the dogwood since the summer
the mink got out of its cage.

Its teeth smelled the chickens
in the yard across the cornfield.
Everyone knows the color of the mud
in which they soon lay.

Everyone knows the nightmare
of the ugly man who rode all night
on the mink's soft brown back.

All day, Grace wrenches the poison ivy
away from the dogwoods. All day,
she dreams she'll ask her husband
If he won't just please leave her alone.

The Poet Digs in the Dirt

Looking for poems, she swallows
the angry dirt her rake has just dug up.

Scowling scratched faces of ghosts
of those she no longer loves and
whom she thinks she buried
years ago stare up at her.

Afraid they will climb up and beat
her and bury her, she runs to the west
woods and crouches silent behind
the fallen oaks.

Maybe the little girl who lives
among the trees will take her hand
and lead her to the river.

Maybe the water will whisper to her.

At Summer's End

Grace slows the mower and stops by the side
of Mother's house. She needs to get home soon
and make supper for the boys before they head
to the barn for evening milking.

She'll come mow around back tomorrow.

Before she goes, she'll sit on the porch with Mother,
just for a few minutes, and have the glass of iced
tea she always fixes.

Her red hair sticks to her face. She watches
the lightning bugs mill around in the weeds
in the garden. She catches one and lets it go.
Another. Lets it go.

As she passes her parents' bedroom window,
she sees Father's ghost, head on chest. He closed
his gray eyes one evening last summer as Mother
was opening a jar of apple sauce in the kitchen.

In bed at home lies the ghost of her Roger,
proud of the boys. She was holding his right hand
the moment when, as quickly as one sweet light
pays court to another, he slid from loving
dreams to silence.

Doing the supper dishes, she used to watch him
through the kitchen window mowing straight
lines from the house to the barn.

The Door

Summer winds and dust squeeze
through the cracks between the slats
of the back door. Shafts of light
whisper to no one in particular.

The poet sits up in bed and wipes
off yesterday's dust. She wonders
where her friends have gone. She
wonders where the chariot of the sun
will take her today.

About the Author

Craig Bruce McVay, of Columbus, Ohio, teaches Classical Mythology at Columbus State Community College. In 2020, Orchard Street Press (Gates Mills, OH) published his first chapbook, *Joy in the Tomb of Hunting and Fishing*.

www.ingramcontent.com/pod-product-compliance
Lightning Source LLC
Chambersburg PA
CBHW030816090426
42737CB00010B/1294